The Relevant Educator

CORWIN CONNECTED EDUCATORS SERIES

The Relevant Educator

How Connectedness Empowers Learning

Tom Whitby

Steven W. Anderson

CORWIN
A SAGE Company

CORWIN
A SAGE Company

FOR INFORMATION:

Corwin

A SAGE Company

2455 Teller Road

Thousand Oaks, California 91320

(800) 233-9936

www.corwin.com

SAGE Publications Ltd.

1 Oliver's Yard

55 City Road

London EC1Y 1SP

United Kingdom

SAGE Publications India Pvt. Ltd.

B 1/I 1 Mohan Cooperative Industrial Area

Mathura Road, New Delhi 110 044

India

SAGE Publications Asia-Pacific Pte. Ltd.

3 Church Street

#10-04 Samsung Hub

Singapore 049483

Copyright © 2014 by Corwin

Printed in the United States of America

A catalog record of this book is available from the Library of Congress.

ISBN 978-1-4833-7171-9

This book is printed on acid-free paper.

Executive Editor: Arnis Burvikovs

Associate Editor: Ariel Price

Production Editor: Amy Schroller

Copy Editor: Janet Ford

Typesetter: C&M Digitals (P) Ltd.

Proofreader: Dennis W. Webb

Cover and Interior Design: Janet Kiesel

Marketing Manager: Lisa Lysne

Certified Chain of Custody
Promoting Sustainable Forestry
www.sfiprogram.org
SFI-01268

SFI label applies to text stock

14 15 16 17 18 10 9 8 7 6 5 4 3 2 1

Contents

Preface

Welcome to the Connected Educators Series.

The past few years have provided momentous changes for educators: Whether it's the implementation of the Common Core State Standards, educational innovations due to technology, teacher and administrator evaluations, or budget cuts, what is clear is that educational reforms come in different shapes and sizes. For many connected educators, one of the invaluable group support systems essential during these times is the professional learning network, also known as our PLN.

Our PLN can provide innovative ideas, current resources, and sound educational practices that stretch our thinking in ways we haven't yet experienced. Equally as important as how a PLN can professionally expand our horizons, it introduces new friends that we look forward to meeting in person. This Connected Educator Series brings together some important members of my PLN. These are educators with a depth of knowledge and level of experience that helps me stay current and up-to-date with my educational practices.

In this series, my book, *Flipping Leadership Doesn't Mean Reinventing the Wheel*, takes the innovative idea of flipping classrooms and presents it at the school leader level, engaging the school community in new and innovative ways. In *Connected Leadership*, Spike Cook shares his experiences moving from a novice to digital leadership and illustrates how other educators can do the same.

Digital experts Steven Anderson and Tom Whitby help increase your digital experience by using Twitter to locate a PLN to engage in daily professional development. In *The Relevant Educator,* Tom and Steven provide a plethora of tools to use, and define each and every one. Using those same tools in their book *The Power of Branding,* Tony Sinanis and Joe Sanfelippo help you to brand your school in order to create a positive focus on the learning happening within the four walls. In his book, *All Hands on Deck,* Brad Currie offers us ways to engage with families and students using old techniques with new innovative approaches.

In *Teaching the iStudent,* Mark Barnes provides insight into the life and mind of the iStudent, and in *Empowered Schools, Empowered Students,* Pernille Ripp focuses on em**power**ing students and teachers. Also in the series, in *Diversity and Connected Learning,* Rafranz Davis shows how equity and diversity is vital to the social media movement, and why that is so important to education as we move forward.

Kristen Swanson from the Edcamp Foundation not only focuses on why the Edcamp model is a new innovative way to provide excellent professional development, but also explains how you can create an Edcamp in your school district in *The Edcamp Model: Powering Up Professional Learning.*

The books in the Connected Educator Series are designed to read in any order, and each provides information on the tools that will keep us current in the digital age. We also look forward to continuing the series with more books from experts on connectedness.

As Michael Fullan has said for many years, technology is not the right driver, good pedagogy is. The books in this connected series focus on practices that lead to good pedagogy in our digital age. To assist readers in their connected experience, we created the Corwin Connected Educators companion website (www.corwin.com/con nectededucator) where readers can connect with the authors and find resources to help further their experience. It is our hope and intent to meet you where you are in your digital journey and elevate you as educators to the next level.

Peter M. DeWitt, EdD @PeterMDeWitt

About the Authors

Tom Whitby is now an Education Social Media consultant. He has served as a contributing Editor for SmartBlog on Education by SmartBrief. Tom retired from public education after serving 34 years as a secondary English teacher. He spent an additional six years as an Adjunct Professor of Education at St Joseph's College in New York. He is the founder of seven educational groups on *LinkedIn*, including the largest "The Technology-Using Professors Group," which is now over 12,000 members strong. He is a co-creator of *#edchat*, an award winning education discussion group on Twitter. He hosts the weekly Edchat Radio Show on the BAM Radio Network. Tom created the *Educator's PLN*, a global Ning site, where over 16,000 educators share and collaborate daily. He participated on the U.S. Department of Education's planning committee for Connected Educator Month in 2013 and 2014. He is an education blogger, *My Island View: Educational, Disconnected Utterances*, and additionally, he is an **EDUTOPIA** blogger. Tom has presented at local, statewide, and national education conferences, including several 140 Character Conferences on Social Media. For the past three years, the Qatar foundation invited him to attend the WISE Conference, an International Education Conference held in Doha, Qatar. He writes about social media in education for several national educational journals, including *Learning and Leading*, the Journal for the International Society for Technology in Education.

 **Steven W. Anderson** is a learner, speaker, blogger, tweeter, and dad. As a former teacher and Director of Instructional Technology, he is highly sought after for his expertise in educational technology integration and using social media for learning. Represented as @web20classroom, he regularly travels the country talking to schools and districts about the use of social media in the classroom and how to better serve students through technology. Steven has been a presenter and speaker at several educational technology conferences, including ISTE, International Society for Technology in Education; ASCD, Association for Supervision and Curriculum Development; FETC, Florida Educational Technology Conference; VSTE, Virginia Society for Technology in Education; and numerous state and local conferences. He is also responsible for helping to create #edchat, a weekly education discussion on Twitter that boasts over 500 weekly participants. For his work with #edchat, Steven was recognized with the 2009 and 2011 Edublogs, Twitterer of The Year Award along with a 2013 Bammy Award, which is recognized worldwide as the Educational Emmy.

From Steven: To my wife, Melissa, and my daughters, Reaghan and Chesney, without y'all I couldn't have done this. And to my Momma, I wrote a book!

From Tom: To my wife Joyce who has endured and supported me in my endless hours of conversing with other people on the computer, and to my daughters Tess and Marissa who have enhanced my learning and patience every day of their lives.

Introduction

Probably more than most other factors, technology advancing social media has had a profound effect on educators and education over the last five years. Numerous articles in journals, newspapers, and magazines, as well as blog posts, support this premise and refer to various components of the connected educator communities and their power to affect change in education through social media collaboration. Social media policies have developed, the common core requires teaching of digital literacy, and most schools have branded themselves with Facebook pages and Twitter accounts. All of this is a response to the effects of social media, specifically in education, and on our society in general.

Collaborative learning has always been a significant component of learning within a face-to-face gathering. With the advent of technology and social media, the previous limits of time and space, which always limited collaboration in the past, are now removed from the equation. This enables educators to collaborate on a global scale regardless of time or location. The effect this has on professional development for educators has underscored the need for all educators to connect in order to communicate, collaborate, curate, and create for personal and professional authentic learning. It has fortified and emphasized the professional and moral imperative educators have to share ideas. Additionally, sharing ideas in such a manner results in a new level of transparency in education.

To be effective in navigating the culture of connectedness, educators need to be more efficient and strategic in their use of the technological skills of the 21st century. These are not only skills educators need to use, but educators are also charged to teach these same skills to their students. Digital literacy is now an integral part of education for teaching and learning, going beyond the application in an education setting to that of the world of work. Strategies and methodologies used for collaborative learning in education are easily carried over to the world of work, enabling lifelong learning to become more than just words in a school's mission statement.

This book examines in depth the various elements that require a level of understanding in order for an educator to develop a professional or personal learning network. It details the impact of social media's effect on education and the skills necessary for an advanced education in this century. It defines and describes what an educator today should look like and how that educator maintains relevance in an ever-changing, technology-driven society.

The openness of social media also adds the element of transparency to the education system. Educators, students, and parents are openly discussing educational experiences. This openness affords educators the ability to examine and analyze on a global level both the successes and failures of educational colleagues. It spearheads reforms through professional development that is driven by the education thought leaders of the profession. This book discusses that impact and offers a perspective on the important space social media occupies moving forward in education.

The significant point is that there is a veritable buffet of social media choices available. Given that reality, this fact can easily overwhelm educators. Within this book, educators can choose from no less than ten social media sites and services to examine and review. It is important to remember that we do not believe that all educators need to be in all these spaces. Each online site or service has its advantages and disadvantages. This book is intended to teach and, as such, illustrates a little of both elements, while driving home the point that no one needs to be an active participant in each and every one of these spaces.

Educators need to be aware of the choices and know where to go to find the best information for their needs.

Connected Learning

I learned more on Twitter in six months than in two years of graduate school.

The connections I've made because I am online are crucial to my success in the classroom.

I don't know what I did before I was connected!

These are statements we hear everyday. Educators from around the world, marveling at the fact that they are connected and how those connections carry a great deal of value to them professionally and personally.

Whether or not you believe in styles of learning, it is a fact that there are several ways that we learn. One way is through collaboration. Collaboration has been a component of education from the beginning; however, the way it evolves has changed dramatically with the advent of digital technology.

Historically, collaboration took place when two or more individuals occupied the same space at the same time and exchanged and revised ideas. There is a well-known saying, "In a room full of smart people, the smartest person is the room!" Now, with today's current technology, there are no boundaries of time or space restricting collaboration. The ability we have to connect and work collaboratively, anytime from anywhere, has elevated collaboration from a limited mode of learning to a more prominent position. Benefiting by various applications, the technology we use for connecting people digitally and virtually has imparted to collaboration the label of "connected learning."

Social media supplies many tools for educators to use in order to make and store their connections with other educators and thought leaders. This storage of connected educators can be accessed and used to personalize learning for any educator. The connected colleagues can serve as resources using face-to-face meetings on Skype, or share their knowledge and links to ideas, websites, blogs, videos, podcasts, white papers, webinars, and educational software programs, such as Google Hangouts, Shindig, or BlackBoard. This network of colleagues is referred to as a PLN or Personal/Professional Learning Network. It enables an individual to contact sources, specifically selected colleagues, to individualize personal learning.

The term PLC refers to a Personal Learning Community, usually formed with a closed community within a school, or a district, or a community of people with a common interest. It is not open to the public, since the applications used for collaboration restrict access to specific people. Educators with access to PLCs may also maintain PLNs.

Although many applications of social media are used to connect people or groups, the backbone of most PLNs relies on Twitter, an online social networking and microblogging service. This site is specifically designed to deliver short messages of 140 characters that can carry links, or addresses (URLs or uniform resource locators) to information. This technology is ideal and indispensable for the needs of educators. Additionally, the ideas shared are in full view of the public eye, which gives a transparency to education that has never before been available. Ideas are exchanged for their worth and not by who delivers them. An idea is an idea—an idea from a teacher is given the same consideration as one from a superintendent. Consequently, titles of individuals are less important when the ideas are the focus. The term "thought leader" has developed to describe those people who are putting forward new ideas in education. Many authors and lead educators are connected and leading education conversations that they offer as sources to everyone. Access to these authors and leaders is available to anyone who contacts them. The culture of the connected community encourages and embraces the idea of sharing: collaboration is the rule and not the exception. This type of access was not possible a decade ago. Imagine if we had the ability to converse with people like John Dewey, the American philosopher, psychologist, and educational reformer, or Benjamin Bloom, an educational psychologist who made contributions to the classification of educational objectives and to the theory of mastery-learning. The technology of social media has enabled these connections, resulting in what is referred to as *connected learning*. It is collaboration through technology.

Since the authors and thought leaders are often the drivers of ideas, and they are connected, the discussions of connected educators advance those faculty meeting discussions by months or longer. The "Flipped Classroom" and "Bring Your Own Device" were ideas discussed in detail in connected circles long before general educators ever heard of the topics. The very discussions and chats currently taking place in the connected community of educators should be the discussions taking place in faculty and department meetings in schools everywhere, but they seldom are.

The connected aspect of learning also offers support to educators. They explore failures, as much as successes. Teachers are validated and respected, which is very important in the current atmosphere where teachers are often vilified and targeted. With connection, common problems are discussed and solutions that have worked for others are offered, examined, and applied. As part of the learning process, failures are also analyzed and discussed. Technology provides educators with a means of connecting never before available. Connected educators have the ability to unite a community of educators to evolve the conversation of education that heretofore has been hijacked by politicians and profiteers, no matter how well meaning the intentions of some. Educators need to overcome their resistance to learning about technology and enter into the culture of connected learning in order to be relevant in our technology-driven society—the very world where we are preparing our kids to live. If we expect to better educate our kids for that world, then it is imperative that we first educate their educators.

Social Media
in Education

WHO IS USING SOCIAL MEDIA?

Whatever the pioneers of social media development had in mind as they developed and expanded the applications of social media, educators view the social media phenomenon differently. As a requisite of a collegial profession, educators always share ideas and sources in collaboration. Social media provides a means to share sources beyond the limits of a school, a district, a state, or even a country. The very sources that educators need are easily shared in a clear and concise form, locally, nationally, and globally. Links leading to websites, documents, white papers, webinars, webcasts, podcasts, videos, posts, articles, as well as online communities, are now continually shared by educators through technology and social media. Face-to-face meetings are accommodated by applications, such as Skype, Shindig, Blackboard, or Google Hangouts. At any time, meetings, lectures, panels, and discussions can all be conducted, and observed, and recorded for later class presentations or archived for professional development.

Administrators are using social media for improving communications with the community. The reality of schools performing well is often unremarked and unrewarded, and good news is rarely disseminated. As a result, branding has now moved beyond advertising and become a term used in education. Schools are developing Facebook pages and Twitter accounts to brand their schools and supply positive messages to the community. Principals and superintendents are posting to their own public blog sites. The telephone calls and occasional parent meetings are being supplemented with texting. Websites are not just developed by schools, but classes as well. All of these growing changes come with a lessening of fears of the Internet, as well as an expansion of social media tools. The understanding of the culture of social media takes some time, but to change any system we need to first change the culture.

The use of technology is no longer a peripheral of choice in education. It is now part of the infrastructure of our society. If we are educating our youth to participate, flourish, and successfully compete in a technology-driven society then they should be learning with the very tools that they will be required to use. In turn, this fact demands that educators are relevant and knowledgeable about the very tools they need to use to teach and model. Educators need to be digitally literate. This is not a passive exercise or one that is taught in books. To learn to swim we need a body of water. Technology provides any learner with a means to connect with others to learn and grow in any area. Social media automatically lends itself as the ideal tool for professional development. Any educator with a degree in educational technology knows that many of the applications and hardware from even a decade ago no longer exist. The simple act of connection enables any educator the ability to maintain relevance in a continually changing and developing profession.

ACCEPTABLE USE POLICY

With the use of social media comes this inevitable statement.

> Social media is bad. It's proliferated with nothing but celebrities and people sharing what they had for breakfast. It has no place in the classroom or as a tool for learning.

Think about the pencil or pen. Over the course of history, many subjects and new things have been introduced that were written about and shared where the public questioned its value or considered it objectionable. But there were never calls to ban quills or graphite. Why is social media any different? As is true with any tool, we have to use it responsibly. And social media is no different. Social media amplifies our voice. Before social media, shared information on a sheet of paper was seen by only a few people, but with social media, that same information can be shared and seen by potentially thousands or millions of people. Take the recent case of a public relations executive who posted some regrettable Tweets just before a flight. By the time she landed, her tweets went viral and she was fired.[1]

The use of social media by educators does not have to be complicated or boxed in by pages of rules. But there are some things to remember if you are an educator who uses social media:

- *Be Honest—Own What You Say.* There is a time and a place for anonymity, but when using social media to learn and grow as an educator, use your own name. Avoid using pseudonyms or fake names.

- *Protect Your Privacy and the Privacy Of Others.* Be smart and discriminate about the information you want others to know about you. Be mindful of the privacy of others; if you don't have permission to share it, don't.

- *Respect Copyright Laws.* It's always good practice to link to original content rather than have it mistaken for your own material. Be respectful of the work others create.

The bottom line for an educator using social media is to be smart. If you wouldn't say it, or do it in person in front of your colleagues, or your school, social media probably isn't the best place for it either.

MYTHS AND MISCONCEPTIONS

As discussed here (and throughout the rest of this book), we speak very positively about social media. It has the potential to empower those that use it, connect us to learning that we once thought was not possible, and communicate our knowledge to the rest of the world. However, there are those in the field who believe social media is something to avoid. Their arguments fall into three main categories.

Social media is evil

If you use social media long enough you hear, or may have already heard, that social media is evil. Cyberbullying, breaking up marriages, breaches of privacy, all are linked to the use of social media. But does that mean that the tool itself is evil? Again, by that logic does that mean that the pencil and paper are evil? Take bullying for example. Students have been writing mean and ugly things to other students since education began. Bullying has been an unfortunate given in schools since way before social media. If the tool is used to hurt or to break the trust of others, that doesn't mean the tool is bad. It all depends on its use.

Bullying via social media can be horrible, but indications are that the specific bullying behavior probably begins in other forms before students continue on to social media outlets. All schools should have bullying prevention plans in place, and that training should start before kids use any social media. Then, the school can set up scenarios to reinforce the plan to emphasize teaching digital responsibility.

Social media is a waste of time

Another argument involves time, or the lack thereof, that is needed to engage in social learning. Constructively spending 20 to 30 minutes a day on social media can open your eyes and your learning to a world of incredible possibilities. However, a quick web search produces plenty of examples identifying people who can't break their social media addiction. There is even a clinic that claims to cure you of your Internet and social media addictions.[2]

Again, just because people become "addicted" doesn't mean the tool itself is bad. We admit that it is easy to get drawn in and before you know it an hour has passed. But the upside of that is to look at what can happened in that hour. Reading blog posts, checking out new tools for the classroom, or engaging in a meaningful chat are all constructive and educational ways to spend your time—now that really is time well spent.

Social media causes a loss of privacy

Since the dawn of the Internet, there has been a push to protect our privacy from exploiting elements. With the use of social media, this exploitation is only amplified. People posting on Facebook that they are going on vacation is seen as an open invitation to the neighborhood thief to take your valuables. The fact is that if you are smart about what information you post, you can avoid mishaps. Also, make certain to note the privacy settings in the social networks you currently use. You *can* control what people see and read about you and *do not* see and read about you.

As is the case with any tool, there are some great examples of correct use of social media and there are some not so great examples. These poor examples don't make the tools bad. We just have to be smart about learning how we can use these valuable social media tools appropriately and responsibly.

The Effects of Culture on Change

SCHOOL CULTURE

Tom: As a professor in education, one of my responsibilities was to observe student teachers in both middle school and high school settings. These constructive visits enabled me to observe not only my students on each visit, but to capture a quick glance of the character of each school. These types of visits continued for years and allowed me to engage teachers and administrators in conversation whenever possible. Every school felt a little different. Often, I spent time in the main office watching the interaction of office staff, administrators, teachers, and even students. If it is true that first impressions are formed with first encounters, then the main office of a school building is a great place to form a lasting impression.

In addition to my higher education experience as a professor, I also worked in several different high schools and middle schools during my career. I entered teaching at a time when New York was faced with a crisis of declining enrollment, which forced a great deal of faculty changes over a considerably long period.

The culture of each school is based on a huge number of factors, similar to an individual's personality. The school culture is as much a collective attitude and belief system as one's personality. Frequently, school policies are developed based on the school's culture. Of course, remember when boys had to tuck in their shirts and girls had the length of their skirts spelled out in a policy? A long time ago, but policies that affect learning are also dependent on the school's culture. In any school, there are hundreds of concerns to be determined, but the priority of the issue and the import of the issue under consideration is usually based on the culture of the school. The collective attitude and beliefs of the decision makers are often based in the culture of the school.

Every school produces a different impression and atmosphere. Obviously, the administrative leadership has a great deal to do with the differences, as well as the structure of each building, but they may not necessarily be the prime influencing factors in every situation. The faculty of the school are also different in many respects and can alter the influence. An older seasoned faculty approaches decisions differently than a younger, energetic, and less experienced group. Traditions also can play a role in the culture of a school. Too often, it can be said that we do things and then, only later, lose sight of why we started to do them in the first place.

This reminds me of a story I heard in a lecture years ago. The speaker told of a family gathering where she was cooking a ham. She cut off about two inches from each side of the ham before placing it in a roasting pan. She asked her mother, who taught her how to cook the ham, why were the ends of the ham cut off? The mother replied that she wasn't sure, but her mother taught that method to her years ago, and she had done it that way ever since. Luckily, the grandmother was still alive, so a phone call was placed. When the grandmother was asked about the method of cutting the ham at both ends, the answer was most revealing about tradition. The grandmother explained that at that time they did not own a big roasting pan, therefore she cut the ends off to make the ham fit in the pan. This story is a great reminder that occasionally we may need to go back and reexamine school policies.

When a school culture is not positive, there are great disadvantages to the school culture. For example, if a school is not supportive of meaningful professional development for its teachers, this can be devastating. If a school is in a pattern that year after year fails to meet district or state requirements, teachers' professional development occurs in workshop sessions during the school year—that is a negative. If a district has an Information Technology (IT) department that operates like the computer police, instead of as technology mentors, that is a negative. If professional development is delivered to teachers based on the bells and whistles of a software application, as opposed to asking teachers how technology can help them reach their specific goals more accurately and efficiently, that is a negative. If a school doesn't support a solid mentoring program for all new teachers, that is a negative. Too many of these negatives add up to a toxic school culture. It is that toxic culture rather than many other singular factors that accounts for almost half of all new teachers leaving the profession within the first five years.

Over the years, I taught students how to use technology in the classroom. All of them were well-educated and well-practiced in the application of technology in education. After school, they were all fired up and ready to go out and change the world. Some of these teachers were fortunate and landed in schools where they were welcomed, mentored, and considered an integral part of the faculty. Others landed in schools where technology was not supported and most teachers were not stretching themselves to learn new things. In other words, the environment seemed more like a job and less like a profession. That group of students did not get the opportunity to change the world. Instead, they were relegated to "a go along to get along" culture of people simply going through the motions. They were definitely victims of a toxic culture.

It is important to shed light on the negatives in education. For many educators, it can create an awareness that for the first time exposes many actions and traditions in their schools as negatives. It is normal for people to hold onto many beliefs, because they were never given pause to examine the origins or the implications of those beliefs. Some ideas may have made sense at one time, but in an ever-changing world many ideas are no longer relevant. In the full light of transparency, we need to have open conversations to examine, vet, modify, expand, or eliminate those things that create a toxic culture. Connected educators who share ideas and experiences are one of the best solutions to improving school culture.

If you are interested in further exploring this subject the works of Anthony Muhammad, a highly respected education consultant and author, are extremely helpful and informative.

INTERNET CULTURE

In my opinion, the culture of the connected education community has developed with a more civil tone than other segments within social media communities. There genuinely appears to be an atmosphere of respect within the education community. People do get passionate about their interests in education, and there are philosophical differences, but for the most part these differences are exchanged with an air of civility.

Since the entire social media world is based on connections and relationships, it is very important to connect and relate to people who will help, challenge, evolve, advance, enhance, and add to your own education philosophy and practice. These influences can and will come from educators from around the world representing a myriad of experiences. Positions and titles seem to be stripped away as ideas are examined and analyzed each on its own merit. It does not matter whether the idea comes from a teacher, a student, an administrator, or a parent. The idea gets the focus and not the contributor.

Many of today's emerging education authors started out as microbloggers on Twitter, moved to blogging, progressed to speaking engagements and producing webinars, and finally wrote a book on their passion. It is impossible to understate the potential for discovering your passion through social media. The constant learning, reflection, refinement, and understanding of various topics within the profession of education challenge us all to be better educators.

Many people who start out in social media assume a position commonly referred to as a "lurker." It is okay to be a lurker in the social media setting. A lurker is a person who lurks to learn. They do not interact, but observe the interactions of others while gaining a sense of the culture and a comfort level to step up to interaction on their own. The interaction and development of relationships greatly increases the learning curve of the learner. Since social media success depends so heavily on interaction and relationships, it is important to follow, connect, and interact with the best people who can offer what it is that you personally need to learn. Typically, what you need to learn is vastly expanded by what you do learn. The more you learn, the more you discover other things that you need to know. All too often, we do not know what it is we really need to know. Social media exposes us to those very needs. Many a lightbulb moment occurs on social media.

CHAPTER

4

Social Media for Professional Development and Professional Learning

BLOGS IN LEARNING

Technology is changing the way relevant information concerning a profession is disseminated. Professional journals are still an important part of the process, but a growing influence in all professions is the emergence of the blog post. Posts are usually short articles written by educators about education. The difference, however, is that the reader may interact directly with the writer. Most blogs allow for comments and offer the reader the ability to argue or agree on points made by the author. Regrettably, there are some administrators and teachers with a previous century mindset, who feel that educators should not openly offer opinions. It always baffles me why anyone would want to stifle the opinions of some of the most educated segment of our society. I am always interested in the thoughts of the very same people I entrust to teach my kids.

Involvement with a blog is a great tool for educators to test their ideas on an audience broader than the members of their department or school building. Of course, not every educator is comfortable putting ideas out in written form for public scrutiny, but more often than not they are comfortable leaving a comment for someone else. When enough comments are placed on a post, it soon prompts a discussion that may trigger other posts on the same topic. These actions all occur in a relatively short period of time without having to wait for another publication date, which is required in the print media.

There is a caution here. Any idiot can put out a blog and almost every idiot does. We must use critical thinking skills to determine the validity of any blogger. Usually time determines whether a blogger is identified as trustworthy or shallow. Once educators are involved reading and commenting on blogs, they begin to weed out the less dependable bloggers. Certain blogs have very large followings, hopefully because they are thoughtful and dependable. Blogs are a great source for generating new ideas, as well as examining or reexamining old ideas.

Many teachers and administrators who maintain blogs report a new sense of rejuvenation for the profession. They report that they reflect more, and focus on changing what doesn't or hasn't succeeded for more relevant approaches in their work. It is not all out with the old and in with the new, but it also reinforces what *is* working—albeit new or old. Blogging is a great sounding board for those willing to try it. Blogging is also sharing and commenting on posts, which in turn allows for sharing to evolve into collaboration as well. Reading blogs should become part of every educator's day. It maintains a sense of relevance. It is one way to keep up with the profession. Any new ideas in education probably show up in blogs long before the print media.

PERSONAL BLOGS

In any discussion about blogging, the positives far outweigh the negatives. Blogging is beneficial for a teacher or a student. Blogging enables you to write for an audience; your words will have meaning, and your ideas will be shared. All of this is empowering. Clarity of thought becomes important. Reflection of ideas takes place before and after you commit to the written word. Readers will read, respond, praise, and criticize, but all of this will help advance your ideas. It will continually amaze you that so many people feel the same as you do, on so many different subjects.

Some educators write professional blogs dealing with professional topics. Others maintain personal blogs, sticking to personal experiences, and sharing ideas. Others combine their professional and personal perspectives into a single blog. Regardless, all blogs represent a personal point of view. Some people will never elect to write a blog, but for those who can, it can be a game changer.

CLASS BLOG

The class blog is not to be feared; it is a perfect way to introduce kids to the world in which they are living in order to understand, analyze, synthesize, and create in a medium of the 21st century. It is an opportunity to teach kids how to properly and respectfully engage people on a platform that uses written expression. Through sharing about the class and all of its accomplishments, the class blog starts the exploration of critical thinking with the kids and also enables the teacher to open the classroom to the outside world. It is risky at first, but the more educated the class becomes at all levels, the easier it becomes for students and teachers to develop digital literacy.

When this figurative window to the class is open, then parents are educated as well in this atmosphere of transparency. Hopefully, the parents are not viewed as adversaries, but partners with their newfound involvement. Parents have always been left out of the education process of their kids with the exception of highly controlled meetings held outside the classroom setting. Class blogs offer the parents a glimpse in real time of their children's experiences and their personal reactions as well. This is a rare glimpse into areas that schools often try to buffer or protect from the parents. Sharing information leads to understanding which gives ownership of education to the parents. If all goes well, a parent adversary group then becomes a parent partner in education.

ZITE, FLIPBOARD, AND RSS FEEDS

Since blog posts are published every hour of every day by thousands of educators, we need a way to curate the best of them in order to glean what we need to personalize our learning. This can be done in a number of ways that save time and cover a great deal of ground. The technology of mobile devices enables educators the ability to carry professional development tools in their pockets.

Zite[1]

Tom—My day begins by opening **Zite** on my iPad. Zite curates blogs in categories of your choosing. Since I am an educator, I selected the category of education. Every morning, I receive on my iPad the most recent and most popular education blogs condensed in a magazine format. If I like what I see in the condensed form, a simple tap on the screen brings up the full post. After reading it, I can either close it out and move on, or tap the screen again to share it with other educators through email, **Twitter**, or **Facebook**. This is a great way for administrators to share posts with faculty. I usually elect to share my preferences with my Twitter followers, which builds up my credibility on Twitter and gains me additional followers daily.

Zite allows me to peruse twenty to thirty blog posts in a very short amount of time, as well as to share them with others. Any submissions I receive that need more attention are stored away using a bookmarking application.

Flipboard[2]

Similar to **Zite**, **Flipboard** allows you to curate blogs and sites by categories and presents them in a very visually appealing magazine format. You can search for specific topics or put in a specific website and add it to your Flipboard.

A feature we really like with Flipboard is the ability to see what others are reading. While we can share what we are reading on our various social networks, we can also choose to make our Flipboards public. This allows others to see what we're reading and curating. We can even choose to include others in our network or out of our network. This is just another way to expand our learning through what we are reading and sharing.

Ironically, during the writing of this chapter, Flipboard purchased Zite from **CNN**. The plan is to eventually merge the two together into one application. The intent is that Flipboard, which is publication-based, and Zite, which is blog-based will blend together into one "deliver it all" application. The applications have been separate companies since they were started about six years ago, but that is yet another example of the rapidity of change in our technology-driven society. The fact that we are connected serves to keep us up to date on these and other changes and is an essential component to becoming a relevant educator.

RSS Feeds

The rate at which new information is posted to blogs and other websites is ever increasing. In the past, in order to follow a favorite site a person might have to check back numerous points in the day to see if new content had been added. Then along came **RSS** or *Really Simple Syndication* that at its core is designed to push new content to you when it is published.

Every blog (and most websites) contain an RSS feed link that can be found somewhere on the site. You can tell the RSS feed by looking for the RSS image. Then using an RSS reader you can subscribe to that site and each time a new post or article is posted, your reader captures it for you.

RSS readers allow you to visit one location to see all of your subscribed content and organize it in a way that is meaningful to you. What sets RSS readers apart from services like Zite or Flipboard is its archiving capabilities. Remember, the amount of new information that is being published every day is growing exponentially. Zite and Flipboard can only capture so much information before old information has to be pushed out in favor of the new. The RSS reader captures everything from the moment you subscribe (and even sometimes before) and allows you to access it. So, while my favorite blogs might post three to four times per day, and many of those posts will show up in Zite or Flipboard, I don't have to worry about missing them.

A Google search for "RSS reader" returns 515,000,000 results. So, needless to say, there are lots of options out there. These software interfaces range from free, no frills services to paid services with lots of customization options. A popular choice for Connected Educators is **Feedly**.[3] Feedly makes it super simple to subscribe to favorite blogs and sites. You don't even need the RSS feed. Type in the website address, or search by title, and Feedly does the work for you. In my opinion, what sets Feedly apart is the suggestions; based on the current feed you are reading, you might see 3 to 5 suggested blogs you are subscribed to that could be of interest. It's a great way to expand on your reading, learning, and network!

OTHER PLACES TO FIND GREAT BLOGS AND CONTENT

There is another site that we use extensively to find education blogs, **Teach 100**.[4] It is a list of the top education blogs ranked for their impact and reach daily. It is easy to find the most popular blogs and receive them with a simple click.

There are a number of blogs that feature educators as guest bloggers. They either encourage educators to contribute posts or they recruit bloggers to address specific themes. Notable blogs of this type include: **Edutopia**,[5] **SmartBlog on Education**,[6] **Edsurge**,[7]

Tech and Learning,[8] **and Education Week.**[9] Additionally, there are sites where any educator may contribute a blog post. **ASCDEdge**[10] is one such site, and it highlights selected posts in the **ASCD SmartBrief**[11]. SmartBrief[12] is an organization that is free to subscribers each week and curates education blogs, condenses them, and e-mails briefs containing several education posts of note. SmartBrief has several content specific education briefs free to educators.

Components of a Personal/Professional Learning Network

WHAT IS A PLN . . . AND WHAT IT ISN'T

Tom: My introduction to a Personal Learning Network, or PLN, came in 2008 from an educator, speaker, author, and 12-year blogger named Will Richardson who introduced the PLN idea to me and to many other educators. At the time, I was not quite sure of what he was talking about, but eventually it all came together. It is very similar to education itself: a person can get the theory about teaching while in a teaching program, but one really becomes a teacher on the job.

Often, the worst advocates for educators developing a PLN are educators who have already developed PLNs. Their successes using a PLN can cause an overexuberance when explaining it to other educators. It is this very enthusiasm for accomplishing so much through a PLN that scares off anyone not familiar with the process. Educators are often intimidated by the list of accomplishments and technology terms that come flooding out from the experienced PLN users. The novice is soon overwhelmed with a feeling of never ever being able to learn all there is to the secrets of the PLN, let alone all that technology. As a result, they immediately decide there is no time nor is there brain space to accomplish any of this stuff.

The idea of a PLN is that it is a network of sources that help an individual personalize his or her learning. Some educators are critical of objectifying people as sources. Although in reality, people are more like collegial sources; they are sources nevertheless. Since this is a personal network, all of the sources are selected by the owner of the PLN. Every PLN is different since each is tailored to the personal learning of its owner. The big questions are: where do I get these sources, and secondly, where do I store all this stuff?

All or any social media applications are used to develop a PLN. The idea is to start slowly so that you can learn as you go. A PLN is not a result of a single professional development (PD) workshop. It is a mindset that enables one to gather sources and save them for as future contacts. The benefit of using social media is that it is as much for the social aspects as it is for gathering information. Relationships are always developed along the way.

Steven: Over the past 5 years, my PLN has grown from one person to include thousands. It has enabled me the opportunity to have conversations with educational thought leaders, such as Alfie Kohn (author and lecturer on education, parenting, and human behavior) and Diane Ravitch (educational policy analyst, and a research professor). I have traveled to Qatar to meet educational leaders from around the world and had the honor of helping teachers all over the globe to connect to one another.

I often get asked about PLNs, and my first advice about PLNs is that the P stands for personal. My PLN looks different from Tom's PLN, and Tom's PLN looks different from the next educator. There are lots of lists and suggestions for specific educators to follow, but ultimately you have to decide the makeup of your PLN and who you want to be a member. No one has the perfect list or the best suggestions. My PLN is very fluid. I make changes all the time, adding new people to follow and unfollowing those that don't provide any value to my learning any more. Make it your own, it is personal, after all.

"Alone we are smart, together we are brilliant!" There is power in numbers and a PLN is powerful.

LINKEDIN

Tom: My starting point in developing a PLN came on LinkedIn. I began connecting with educators and found that I was very limited in my communication by the application I was using. I then discovered that I could start a group on LinkedIn.[1] I started a group called the Technology-Using Professors Group.[2] I wanted ideas for the higher education courses I was teaching. It seemed that many others were looking for the same connections. That group is still going strong and numbers over 11,000 college professors from around the world constantly engaged in discussion. LinkedIn is the professional's social network. I think of it as a Rolodex of educators. It supplies a great deal of background on individuals for personal contacts.

TWITTER[3]

Tom: As successful as I was at gathering sources on LinkedIn, my real PLN involvement was yet to begin. More and more, I recognized that the discussions on LinkedIn referred to the Twitter application. I had a Twitter account, but I was not really using it. I asked someone to explain it again to me and that is when a lightbulb appeared over my head. I began to gather up and follow as many educators as I could on Twitter. As I grew my sources, my twitter stream began to fill up with links to websites, documents, posts, webinars, podcasts, interviews, and videos all dealing with aspects of education or subjects that I could carry over to my classes. It was a smorgasbord of information. Many educators use Twitter as the backbone of their PLN. It is the quickest way to get information, and it goes out on a global scale.

FIGURE 5.1 Tom's First Tweet

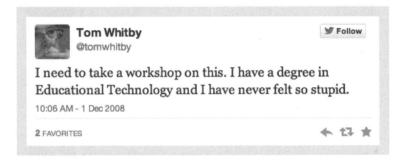

Tom Whitby
@tomwhitby
🐦 Follow

I need to take a workshop on this. I have a degree in Educational Technology and I have never felt so stupid.

10:06 AM - 1 Dec 2008

2 FAVORITES

Steven: I signed up for my first Twitter account in November 2008. I had heard about Twitter here and there and decided to sign up. I never had a specific strategy; I just followed random people. By December, I gave up and deleted my account.

In the meantime, I started my blog and began reading other blogs by educators. Again, I started to see Twitter creeping into some posts. Then, I read a post from an educator in Missouri and she mentioned a wiki that had invited others and was tweeting educators to share their information. I signed up again, and began to follow ten educators—that made all the difference.

By locating a core group of educators that I wanted to follow, I received tweets that I was interested in, or tweets that taught me something. I finally found the real value in Twitter.

FIGURE 5.2 Steven's First Tweet

Steven W. Anderson 🔽 Follow
@web20classroom

Looking for ideas for a new blog posting...any one have
any great educational technology ideas they want to share?

9:13 AM - 25 Feb 2009

↩ ⟲ ★

Tom and Steven: The question we are often asked is how do you find others to follow? There are many more connected educators tweeting today than when we began on Twitter. Consequently, finding educators to follow is a bit easier, but it is still very daunting.

In the blogs you read, look for Twitter handles. If you enjoy the content that someone writes, you may like the tweets they post. From there, you can see who they are conversing with or retweeting. This is one way and a fairly easy way to expand the list of people you follow. Also, prolific tweeter Jerry Blumengarten's (@cybraryman1[4]) PLN page[5] has a collection of lists of twitter users, broken down by grade and/or subject and by general topic.

CHATS

Twitter is also the best way to move and expand your own information. Tweets can drive traffic to your website or blog post. You can express ideas or opinions for instant feedback. You can ask questions and elicit responses from all over the world. It is also the means by which hundreds of education chats take place in real time, seven days a week. Chats are discussions that cover various topics in education and are open to anyone who elects to participate. The chats themselves cover a great deal of ground, but after reflection, it is my sense that the blog posts resulting from the chats are where the real gold is found. After people give thought to the topics and hear the objections as well as the accolades then the ideas begin to gel. The best part is that everyone gets to take ownership of the process.

#Edchat was not the first chat on Twitter, but it was the most successful and continues to be the longest running chat. There are two #edchats[6] available every Tuesday, one scheduled at noon and another at 7:00 pm Eastern Standard Time (EST). Each chat covers a different education topic. The topics are determined by a popularity poll conducted two days prior to each chat. Since the introduction of #edchat, there are now hundreds of chats dealing with every possible topic: grade levels, subjects, special education, technology, and language groups.

A word of caution: Twitter is not the best application to use to participate and follow a chat. TweetDeck[7] and Hootsuite[8] both allow the user to create columns to more easily follow specific hashtags (#)(a **hashtag** is a way to unite global Tweets around some particular topic), individuals, or groups. An application specifically designed to follow and participate in chats is Tweetchat.[9]

Please visit the companion website to see a list of weekly Twitter chats[10] as of March 1, 2014, compiled by @Thomascmurray @cevans 5095 and @cybraryman1.

PODCASTS

The popularity of podcasts seems to come and go. A few years ago, loads of folks were listening to podcasts and creating their own. Then the excitement seemed to wane, but now podcasts are on the rise again.

Podcasts truly allow for mobile learning, anywhere. The connected educator can load his or her iPod with hours of podcast conversations and elect to listen on the commute to work, during planning, or even waiting at the doctor's office. Some podcasts are short and easy to digest in a small amount of time, while others are an hour long and foster sharing and deeper conversations.

The BAM! Radio Network[11] has podcasts for all types of topics. There is something for everyone from #Edchat[12] Radio, to a channel dedicated to the exploration of the flipped classroom, to a channel on how to get parents more involved in the classroom. You can subscribe to the podcast feed or listen right on the site.

SKYPE AND GOOGLE HANGOUTS

There are two applications that put a face to digital collaborative learning. **Skype**[13] and **Google Hangouts**[14] enable educators to visually see and interact with the persons they selected for their communications. These sites allow an educator the ability to bring an expert on any topic into the classroom. Each site has its own advantages. Skype has limits on the number of participants, but it is a very stable platform that focuses on the main speaker on the screen. Google Hangouts allows for multiple users to view each other, and screen sharing allows presentations to be enhanced with PowerPoint. Both of these applications permit educators new to the process to bring collaborative learning in line with whatever version they are most comfortable with and understand. They both also serve well in engaging audiences in class or group situations.

WEBINARS

As we have seen, connected educators use multiple methods to communicate and collaborate. Certainly, Skype and Google Hangouts allow for informal collaboration. We use them all the time to work on various projects or to just catch up with each other. There are, however, more formal learning opportunities available through the use of webinars.

Webinars utilize various web-based platforms that countenance presenters and participants to learn while participating from anywhere in the world. Features vary from platform to platform, but in their essence they are the same. They permit anyone to connect with audio (and sometimes video) to watch a presentation. Many have areas for participants to interact with each other through chat or messages, and presenters can share documents and other materials as well.

Many organizations offer free webinars on a wide variety of topics to extend the learning that many connected educators are seeking. **Edweb.net**[15] is a large community of educators that offers weekly webinars on various aspects of the education profession. Also, the large **Classroom 2.0**[16] community hosts a weekly webinar on Saturdays where members of the connected educator community present and share.

Along with the several communities that are offering webinars, independently organized virtual conferences are being generated more frequently. **The Reform Symposium,**[18] organized entirely by educators, is a 24-hour, 3-day event that presents webinars in multiple languages on multiple subjects. The **Global Education Conference**[19] is similar, but it lasts an entire week. The newly formed **School Leadership Summit**[20] focuses its sessions on leadership issues facing school and district administrators.

CHAPTER
6

National and Statewide Education Conferences

For decades, professional education organizations have conducted annual conferences highlighting professional development workshops in their area of expertise. Originally organized and planned by educators, many of these conferences have grown beyond the capabilities of full-time educators. Thus, many are now planned and managed by professional conference organizers. Distant locations, travel and living accommodations, the expense of substitute teachers, and the high cost of registration for these conferences limit the number of people who can attend from any given district. Often, it is the administrators who attend because they have the available budget, and many repeat their attendance year after year. In reality, only a small percentage of the teacher population ever gets to attend these conferences.

The primary intent of these conferences is to develop workshop sessions featuring the latest and greatest educational information to share with the attendees who (theoretically) then go back and share this new information with their districts. The downside to this approach is that given the amount of required planning then, the RFP, or Request for Proposal, needs to be submitted eight to twelve months before the actual conference date. Another drawback is the number of workshops available far exceeds the ability of attendees to attend.

The formula and format for these conferences have remained relatively unchanged for many years. With the advent of connected education, there have been a number of obvious changes to the conference format, causing both positive and negative effects.

MARKETING THE CONFERENCE THROUGH CONNECTIONS

Education conferences take a year to plan, which gives planners time to create websites specifically designed for the conference. Many create **Ning** sites (an online platform for people and organizations to create custom social networks) so that a community of educators can interact and plan for the upcoming event. As keynote speakers and events are secured, the news is released via Twitter and through these Ning sites. The idea is to create a buzz or generate interest about the conference with the expected audience—connected educators.

Hashtag (#) Backchanneling

Using Twitter, educators can devise hashtags to create a synchronous chat about any subject. Every conference now creates its own hashtag for educators to tweet out their conference experience. The hope is that the posts will be positive and create a buzz among those connected educators who could not attend in person. This is a 21st century form of connected marketing.

Hashtags also play an important role in individual sessions. As educators participate in sessions, they tweet out their impressions, as well as the words and ideas from the presenter. This amount of transparency puts a greater responsibility on presenters to be prepared and relevant. A poor presentation is a flirtation with public humiliation.

This entire process enables educators who could not attend the conference to attend virtually. They respond to tweets from sessions. They receive pictures and videos from their connected colleagues of sessions, keynotes, and thought leaders. Connected educators extend the face-to-face conference to many more educators than just those in attendance.

Social Media Venues at Conferences

Most conferences are now recognizing and accommodating the connected educator. A Bloggers Café is now visible and even highlighted at most conferences. It is a virtual lounge area to attract bloggers, not only for the bloggers to meet and connect, but also for the educators who follow them to be able to connect face to face. Some examples of areas in conferences that are provided for connected educators to gather for the same reason are The PLN Plaza, The Digital Zone, and the Social Media Center.

Conferences and Connectedness

Connected educators are continually discussing education; the connected discussions are often in advance of education discussions in faculty or department meetings. The thought leaders in education are often blogging and tweeting about education topics before these topics gain acceptance by an entrenched and slower education system. In the past, a frustration faced by many educators was that their creative juices flowed freely during the conference, but immediately after the conference there was no one who had a similar experience that they could share with. The mere fact of being connected enables those connections and creativity to continue and expand far past the date of the conference.

Conferences providing sessions that are prepared eight to twelve months in advance are no longer the draw they once were. The timeliness of connected learning is driving a different timetable and pushing for more relevant topics and better prepared presenters. If the format of the conventional conference does not respond to the changing needs of educators, then educational conferences will surely outlive their original purpose.

Moving forward conferences embrace the connected educator movement to gain more visibility among the majority of educators who in the past were left looking in from the outside. The idea that those in attendance can easily share what they are learning with those who could not attend is a great step forward in public relations for the state and national education organizations. The ability of educators to develop relationships at conferences and maintain them as ongoing throughout the year is a big addition to any conference experience.

THE EDCAMP AND UNCONFERENCE MOVEMENT

While many national and statewide conferences provide a vast amount of resources for educators, there is a growing feeling that many professional learning needs are not being met at these conferences or from the professional development provided at the district or local level. Social media has certainly provided a level of learning that aims to meet these needs, but many educators are seeking more.

In 2009, a group of educators in the Philadelphia area attended a BarCamp[1] event. Founded by computer programmers, BarCamps are ad-hoc gatherings in an open environment that allow the programmers time to share and learn from each other. Excited by the possibilities that the BarCamp model provided, the educators founded Edcamp Philly[2] in May of 2010. The idea was simple. Provide a space and a time where educators could gather and talk about whatever was of interest to them. There is no set agenda, speakers, or topics. The only thing decided ahead of time was the length of the sessions, and even that was flexible.

Edcamp Philly and the Edcamp model proved to be so popular that Edcamps began popping up all over the country. By the end of 2013, there were nearly 500 Edcamps in almost every state and in several countries around the world.[3] Typically held on a Saturday, it is not unusual to find several Edcamps being held simultaneously across the globe.

Steven: Edcamps tap in to the desire of educators to be in control of their own professional development. As the co-organizer of EdcampNC, I know firsthand the excitement people have when they attend one of these events. The participants dictate what they learn, and how they learn it. There is a great deal of power in that. Participants of an Edcamp can take multiple paths during the day. They can choose to present on a topic that is of interest to them. They can propose a topic they feel needs to be talked about, but want the wisdom of the group during the conversation. Or they can simply participate, attending sessions, contributing to conversations, tweeting, or just listening.

What sets Edcamps apart from the national or state conferences, aside from the participant-driven nature of the event, are several other factors. First, Edcamps are inexpensive for the organizers to put on with a general cost of just a few hundred dollars, and therefore participation is free. Additionally, no vendors are in attendance at Edcamps. Some organizations and websites may donate door prizes, but vendors do not sponsor Edcamps. Finally, there is a mutual understanding or guiding principle at Edcamps called the "Rule of Two Feet." The rule is that if you are in a session that isn't meeting your needs, you find another that does, even if it is in the middle of the session. At many national and state conferences, leaving during a session might be considered rude, but it is an accepted part of the Edcamp experience. These events are participant-driven and founded on the idea that they are creating environments for educators to be in control of their own learning.

A variation on the Edcamp model is the Unconference. Similar to Edcamps, the Unconference provides the opportunity for participants to have some say in what types of sessions make up the event, but there is usually more structure, and many Unconferences have vendor or organizational influence. One such popular occurrence is the Hack Education[4] or ISTE Unplugged event held before the ISTE conference every year. During this one-day event, participants gather in the morning and propose session topics. A vote is then taken to determine which sessions make the cut.

Whether you elect to participate in an Edcamp, or an Unconference, the benefits are clear. Educators are seeking out choices when it comes to their professional development. They want to be in control of their learning and decide how, when, and where they learn about topics that will have the most impact on their teaching and their classroom. Edcamps and Unconferences provide that level of control and give educators another option when it comes to their professional learning.

SOCIAL MEDIA EXPANDS ANY EDUCATION CONFERENCE EXPERIENCE

Connected educators have the ability to incorporate their connectedness into almost every aspect of a standard education conference. Conferences are announced through social media, and social media traffic is channeled to websites announcing, organizing, scheduling, and registering each aspect of a conference. Contacts can be made, accommodations can be arranged, and session schedules can be predetermined. Social media is used during conferences to share session ideas with the majority of educators who could not be there in person. Probably the most important aspect of social media in conferencing is the ability that connected educators have to continue relationships developed at the conference. Staying connected to people who shared ideas at a conference is enabled and enhanced with technology in a way never before afforded to educators.

Innovative ideas and best practices have always been the staple of education conferences. However, the audience benefitting from the conferences was limited to the attendees who arrived at conferences as explorers and not prepared participants. In the world of connected educator communities, the benefits of conferencing can be shared out many more times, amplifying the influence of the conference regardless of what form the conference takes. Most importantly, the very creative juices stirred up in individuals from a conference may continue to flow through connected relationships long after the conference is over.

Social Media Communities

For quite a long period of time, there has been an application that allowed a user to create an online community of like-minded people for free. It is called Ning.[1] It spawned a huge amount of sites that enabled organizations and hobbyists alike to gather together a group of people to share articles, blog posts, videos, discussions, and pictures. They could even form groups within the group. The Ning sites began to multiply quickly enough that it soon began to impose a charge for what was once a free service. After all, Ning is a business—and we all know there are very few free things in business.

Tom: I was teaching education methods courses in a small college in New York when I discovered the Ning platform. I had accumulated many digital sources for my students to use in their studies, and was sending them daily e-mails, but I quickly determined that was not efficient. I created a Ning site and called it *Methods Matters*. I was able to store sources on it, which was great, but I was also able to have my students blog on that site as well. It afforded me an opportunity to get them to openly reflect and share with their colleagues in a safe environment. It also enabled students to interact on these reflections with comments. The site was not public, it was only open to my students and certain other faculty. Students began to add their own sources. Discussions in class became extensions of those that initiated on the Ning platform. I was very pleased with the outcome.

It was then that I decided to create a site for all educators to connect and collaborate and mentor each other while in the process of connecting and developing a PLN. I called it The Educator's PLN.[2] It is still thriving today with over 16,000 educators worldwide, and as of this date, educators can find over 1,000 education videos, discussions, groups, blogs, tutorials, websites, and most importantly other educators from around the world with whom they can choose to connect.

Steven: My first contact with a social media driven community was when I signed up for Classroom 2.0 shortly after I joined Twitter. I heard several educators reference conversations at that site, so I decided to check it out. At that time (March 2009), it was the largest place for educators to gather to carry out asynchronous conversations. What I found there were groups dedicated to various subject areas and themes, threaded discussion forums where users could ask questions, seek answers, and offer advice, and a place where every Saturday there were live webinars for learning.

Being a member of Classroom 2.0 and other social media communities allows me to go deeper with my thoughts with others. While Twitter provides me a platform for building and growing my Personal Learning Network (PLN), it may not be the best fit for other users. Social media communities like Classroom 2.0 provide a sense of community without the real-time anxiety some feel when communicating with the synchronous nature of Twitter.

A LIST OF SOME OF THE MORE ACTIVE COMMUNITIES

ISTE14[3] Ning (www.iste.org/)

ASCDedge (professional networking community)

New York State Association of Computers and Technology in Education (NYSCATE, www.nyscate.org/)[4]

Classroom 2.0 (previously referenced in Chapter 5) Edutopia Groups[5]

English Companion-Ning[6]

The National Council for Social Studies-Ning[7]

The Synapse-Ning (Biology Educators)[8]

TechinEDU-Ning (Technology Integration in Education)[9]

Flipped Learning Network-Ning (Teacher Vodcasting and Flipped Classroom Network)[10]

EFL Classroom 2.0-Ning[11]

One platform that is larger than Ning and hosts the most communities is **EdWeb**. It is a community free to educators, but it is paid for through advertising. In addition to the usual resources provided, EdWeb also provides a great number of webinars. These are seminars presented through the web, or webinars. This is a relatively old format used for professional development that is now digitized for this century.

From the EdWeb site:

edWeb.net is a highly acclaimed professional social and learning network that has become a vibrant online community for exceptional educators, decisionmakers, and influencers who are on the leading edge of innovation in education.

edWeb members are teachers, faculty, administrators, and librarians at K–12 and post-secondary institutions. edWeb is a place where educators who are looking for ways to improve teaching and learning can gather and share information and ideas with peers and thought leaders in the industry.

Some schools are using **Edmodo**[12] to build closed communities within their districts. It is a great way to introduce collaboration in a controlled way, but it does rather defeat the purpose of global collaboration, as well as open transparency. The comparison is like putting a set of training wheels on a kid's bike, but never getting to the point of removing them.

The Internet holds a vast number of sources for educators; unfortunately, most are simply unaware of the majority. A simple list of education communities and a quick Google search should get any educator started down the path of digital enlightenment. Exploration is the fun part of learning for many. A curiosity of what may be out there in the Ethernet is a driving force in the exploration of the Internet for any serious learner. Relevance is just an add-on to whatever knowledge we obtain through this learning. As educators, we must engage in the life-long learning that we profess to our students daily. In order to be better educators, we must first be better learners.

CHAPTER

8

Getting Started

B uilding a PLN is not a race, but a process. Since its goal is to personalize learning, the development of this network depend on how the learner learns, adapts, and executes the methods needed to move to the next step. No matter how advanced one gets into the process, there is always going to be a next step. The nature of technology evolves at a rapid rate, so inevitably we are always trying to catch up. Accept that you will never learn it all, but you can learn what you need. Anyone who is standing still in a tech-driven world, is actually falling behind, minute by minute.

Tom: As an educator I received my master's degree in Educational Technology in 1991. Since that time, not a single piece of hardware or software that I used to earn that degree is in use today. Technology and its effects does not wait for us to comprehend it. To keep up, we need to keep learning—and that takes time.

The key to a great PLN is not the number of people you follow, but the quality of those you follow. It is important to connect with people willing to share: you get to choose, and if you do not think you made a correct choice, you get to drop that choice and move onto another. This control holds true for whatever social media platform you select. Always keep in mind that the quality of the information you get, as a professional educator, is directly attributable to the quality of the educators that you follow.

I elected Twitter to serve as the foundation of my PLN. It is the easiest platform to access and maintain anywhere and at anytime. Mobile devices carry professional development directly to you, wherever and whenever you decide to engage. A great starting point is to open a Twitter account.

Twitter is not as complicated as some people make it. If you have a twitter account, it is based on two things. People that you follow, and people who follow you. If you have ten followers and you put out a tweet, then only those ten followers see it, and you will only see the tweets of the people that you follow. Therefore, for the sake of learning, that means that who you follow is much more important than who follows you. Don't get caught up in the "my followers' list is bigger than your followers' list" game. Numbers are for the ego and not for learning. Ego is nice, but learning is what we seek.

With the addition of hashtags (#) on twitter, tweets can go beyond your followers. A tweet with a hashtag added goes out to anyone following that hashtag. #Edchat is a hashtag that when added to a tweet gets that tweet to thousands of educators who follow that subject specifically. #Edchat is the most commonly used hashtag to attach to tweets dealing with education topics. Almost any hashtag boosts the range of any tweet. You can follow specific hashtags by creating columns for them in Tweetdeck or Hootsuite, both described in Chapter 5. On Fridays, a very unique hashtag is used on #edchat, #FF. It stands for Follow Friday. It is attached to tweets that recommend some very good people to follow on Twitter. It is a great way to build your PLN with endorsed people of value. These are people vetted by educators and recommended to you. Remember, with #FF recommendations, Take'm and Make'm.

Most education bloggers are also Twitter users. Usually, you can follow a blogger from a Twitter "Follow Me" icon posted on their blog site. As you begin to follow more and more individuals, you note that your Twitterstream begins to carry more and more links to education sources. You can also identify those educators who are more in line with your specific interests. If you examine the Twitter profiles of people you admire, you will discover that they may have lists of people that they follow. You can simply click on each of the people on that list and you will be following them as well. Remember, you can *unfollow* anyone at anytime without concern of notification.

With each link sent by educators you may be exposed to previously unknown sources. Websites, documents, webinars, podcasts, webcasts, interviews, and videos will all flow through your Twitterstream. They will lead you to more sites and sources every day. The time you spend depends on what you can invest. Twenty minutes a day is a small investment of time to reap sources that save you that amount of time and more as you learn about and develop more efficient methods for the classroom. You may discover a rejuvenated, more reflective approach to your present education philosophy. Certainly, the influence of direct access to education thought leaders has a significant effect on your education relevance. The fact that so many educators on your PLN have such varied experiences with technology in education is the reason to use them as a source for all your questions about technology in education.

Once the Twitter PLN is in place, it begins to take you to other applications, but not all at once. You determine what you need to know, and when you need to know it. You control your own learning. The PLN is the spigot that you can turn on and off when you need it; you control the strength of the flow. You will meet many other educators developing relationships in this collaborative environment. Remember to give as much, if not more, than you get. Respect is the key to great collaboration. Your colleagues will give you as much respect as you afford them.

CHAPTER
9

The Connected
Educator

All connected educators are collaborative, but not all collaborative educators are connected. Technology is the difference. We have always had face-to-face connections for collaboration. It is technology that has taken collaboration to another level and removed the boundaries of time and space so that educators can collaborate locally or globally without regard to a clock or schedule. Collaboration can be synchronous or asynchronous.

It is this necessary component of technology that has slowed the progress of connected learning among educators. At the very least, there is the requirement of a basic understanding of social media applications in order for educators to use collaborative skills digitally. That understanding does not come passively. It requires an effort to learn the basics of social media as well as the corresponding culture. It is not a difficult transition for someone willing to learn, but many see it as a drain on time required for other endeavors. It is also outside the comfort zone for many. These two factors alone are enough to prevent a great many educators from becoming connected.

TIME KEEPS ON SLIPPING . . .

The fact is that once an educator is connected, the time it takes to connect is often more than compensated by the discovery of more efficiencies through technology. The difficulty of exiting a comfort zone is made easy by personalizing what needs to be learned. Every educator can control what they want to learn and the time they want to spend on the process. Twenty minutes a day should be enough for any educator to move forward. However, recognize that once that time is invested, many educators find a need to willingly spend more time learning. It is a matter of discovering that the rewards of connecting outweigh the investment of time. The ideas and methods acquired through connections can potentially save time and improve instruction. Time spent online becomes time well spent as an educator. In truth, leaving the comfort zone is often a reintroduction to lifelong learning and rejuvenating to many educators. It offers a fresh view on many topics that may have lost relevance, but now reexamined within a technology-driven culture.

As Twitter users we get asked often, "Do you ever sleep?" Sure we do. (Steven: Although as the father of two young children, I wonder sometimes!) Both of us have been engaged in online communities and social media for over 5 years. We've learned how to manage our time. But the use of social media is such an integral part of our learning and our professional growth that it no longer seems unusual to us. Google is a great resource, but we trust the knowledge of our PLNs much more. As a result, sending a tweet, or posting to a message board is something that we do regularly. From the outside, this time may seem like a waste, but to the Connected Educator it is crucial.

WHY IS SHARING SO HARD?

Steven. Think back to the first time you stepped into a classroom. You were probably fresh out of college or an internship with lots of ideas. If you were like me, you couldn't wait for the school year to start because you wanted to try all the things you had learned.

I remember my first years. Teaching science, I read as much as I could about being a science teacher. I attended conferences whenever I could. I experimented (like any good scientist) with different methods and ways of teaching. My principal took notice. She asked me to share what was working in my classroom with some colleagues. I got a very cold reception. Veteran teachers, who were really good at teaching, perceived me as seeking some kind of glory. I was told by one teacher that good teachers don't share.

I grappled with the idea of not sharing. How could that be the best way? It seemed to me that if there was something working in my classroom, why wouldn't I share it so that others could learn too? I would expect the same from my colleagues.

Sharing is the basis of collaboration, and collaboration is the basis for connectedness. There is no real collaboration without sharing. Some educators view sharing as bragging, and bragging is a negative in the education community. Educators with this perspective probably cannot fully embrace the idea of connected learning. If the goal of education is learning, then educators should have a moral imperative to share.

Consider how we would feel about a researcher who discovered a cure for cancer, but failed to share those results with others. In sharing those results, is that researcher bragging? What other researchers' work could have been advanced with that information? How much time could have been saved in regard to other related research? There is a moral imperative to share in communities. Sharing is not bragging, but it does promote learning.

Being a Connected Educator allows all of us to share what works with teaching and learning and what might not work. It allows us to grow and learn from each other. Alone we are smart, but together we are brilliant. The fact that connected educators use social media allows their voice to be amplified, to influence many more educators than ever before, and to have far-reaching effects on the classroom and on learning.

WHAT DOES A CONNECTED EDUCATOR LOOK LIKE?

A Connected Educator embodies a mindset rather than represents someone who does specific things in specific ways. Few connected educators exhibit all of the qualities and characteristics of a connected educator, but they do have some common beliefs.

A Connected Educator

- believes in sharing and collaboration;
- uses technology and its connection to other educators to learn and teach;
- practices and models lifelong learning, which is often a concept professed to students as a goal of education;
- uses the tools of technology to personalize his or her professional development;
- is a relevant educator, willing to explore, question, elaborate, and advance ideas through connections with other educators;
- if not comfortable with new technology, still shows a willingness to explore its use;
- views failure as part of the process of learning; and
- may put creation over content, and relevance over doctrine.

A Connected Educator may exhibit all or some of these qualities, but the real commonality of connected educators is the use of technology to collaborate in the pursuit of lifelong learning. These educators are active participants on Twitter, write regularly in their blogs, and take part in webinars to expand their knowledge and/or contribute to online communities to help others grow. They realize that learning can and does happen anywhere and they want to be a part of it wherever it occurs.

In a society where analog has been replaced by digital and the country's infrastructure is being retooled and rebuilt to accommodate information technology, technology plays and will continue to play an ever-growing role in our lives. We are preparing citizens for a world that continuously evolves technologically. We, as educators, need to understand that dynamic and evolve at a pace that at least keeps us from falling behind. The tools of communication, collaboration, and creation have radically changed and will continue to transform. These are the very tools we are preparing our children to use in order to thrive and compete in their evolving world. The Connected Educator is a model for all educators as we move forward. A Connected Educator is as much a learner as a teacher. A Connected Educator is digitally literate and progressing as needed to adapt to the changes that will inevitably occur. A Connected Educator is relevant in a world of rapidly paced change.

Additional Resources and Connected Educator Vocabulary

Chapter Reference Guide

Chapter 2

1. *Fired PR executive apologizes for AIDS in Africa tweet.* Retrieved from http://bit.ly/plnmistake

2. *First U.S. rehab center for Internet addiction opens its doors.* Retrieved from http://bit.ly/plninternetrehab

Chapter 4

1. **Zite**—A site that curates blogs into a magazine format. Available at http://zite.com

2. **Flipboard**—Curates magazine articles into a magazine format. Available at http://flipboard.com

3. **Feedly**—An RSS feed that curates blogs of your choosing. Available at http://feedly.com

4. **Teach 100**—A website that ranks over 400 education blogs daily. Available at http://teach.com/teach100

5. **Edutopia**—Practical classroom strategies and tips from real educators, as well as lesson ideas, personal stories, and innovative approaches to improving your teaching practice. Available at http://www.edutopia.org/blogs

6. **Smartblog on Education**—Educators guest blog for SmartBrief. Available at https://smartblogs.com/category/education/

7. **Edsurge**—A website with news and blogs about education technology. Available at https://www.edsurge.com/

8. **Tech & Learning**—A digital magazine focusing on tech tools and learning. Available at http://www.techlearning.com/Blogs

9. **Education Week**—The latest articles and guest posts on education delivered as a digital journal. Available at http://www.edweek.org/ew/section/blogs/index.html

10. **ASCDEdge**—A community of educators contributing blogs, videos, and discussions dealing with education. Available at http://edge.ascd.org

11. **ASCD Smartbrief**—A weekly e-mailed publication providing top education posts of the week. Available at http://bit.ly/plnascdsmartbrief

12. **SmartBrief**—A list of free education publications consisting of education blogs. Available at http://bit.ly/1nyhpum

Chapter 5

1. **LinkedIn:** Business networking site for those interested in professional occupations. Several education groups reside on this site. Accessible at http://linkedin.com

2. **Technology-Using Professors Group:** A LinkedIn group for professors who use technology in class. Accessible at http://linkd.in/1kIpoXe

3. **Twitter:** A social media application that allows participants to send messages to others with a maximum of 140 characters. Accessible at http://twitter.com

4. **Cybraryman1:** The Twitter handle of Jerry Blumengarten, a retired teacher and frequent chat moderator who maintains a website containing many pages of sources for educators. Accessible at http://twitter.com/cybraryman1

5. **Cybraryman's PLN Page:** Building a PLN. My PLN Stars. Accessible at http://cybraryman.com/plnstars.html

6. **#Edchat Archival site:** The #Edchats from the early days until today have been archived on this website. Accessible at http://edchat.pbworks.com

7. **TweetDeck:** Third-party Twitter application that allows you to better organize Tweets. Accessible at http://tweetdeck.com

8. **Hootsuite:** Similar to TweetDeck, this is a third-party Twitter application that allows you to better organize Tweets. Accessible at http://hootsuite.com

9. **Tweetchat:** A website that allows you easier participation in a Twitter chat by auto inserting the hashtag and slowing down the stream. Accessible at http://tweetchat.com/

10. **Weekly Twitter Chats:** A regularly scheduled time for Twitterers, using a common hashtag, to discuss and debate education topics and issues. Accessible at http://bit.ly/offi cialchatlist

11. **Bam Radio Network:** A website and podcasts dedicated to informing the public about emerging trends in education. Home of #Edchat Radio. Accessible at http://www.bamradio network.com/

12. **#Edchat Radio Show:** iTunes podcast list of #Edchat Radio shows to download Accessible at http://bit.ly/1oG Zkcc

13. **Skype:** Free video calling program. Great tool for in-class face-to-face collaboration. Accessible at http://skype.com

14. **Google Hangouts:** Another free, video chatting service, allowing up to 10 concurrent users, screen sharing, and more. Accessible at http://bit.ly/plngooglehangouts

15. **EdWeb:** A community supported by advertising for educator collaboration. Owned and managed by Lisa Schmucki, this site provides free webinars for educators. Accessible at http://home.edweb.net/

16. **Classroom 2.0:** This is a Ning (online platform for people and organizations to create custom social networks) community founded and managed by Steve Hargadon for educators to collaborate on the latest methods, pedagogy, and technology in education. Accessible at http://www.classroom20.com/

17. **Classroom 2.0 LIVE:** This is a site that supports Classroom 2.0 with LIVE webinars free to educators every Saturday. Accessible at http://live.classroom20.com/

18. **Reform Symposium:** The Reform Symposium, the Electric Conference, this is a website that supports the Reform Symposium Free Online **Conference** (RSCON), an annual 3-day worldwide conference free to educators, and delivered over the Internet. Accessible at http://reformsymposium.wordpress.com/

19. **Global Education Conference:** The Global Education Conference is a collaborative, inclusive, worldwide community initiative involving students, educators, and organizations at all levels. Accessible at http://www.globaleducationconference.com/

20. **School Leadership Summit (Administrator 2.0):** A Ning community for administrators. Accessible at http://admin20.org/page/summit

Chapter 6

1. **Barcamp:** Provides an explanation of Barcamps, which was a precursor to Edcamps. Accessible at http://en.wikipedia.org/wiki/BarCamp

2. **Edcamp Philly:** A Ning community that changes each year to introduce and inform people of the latest rendition of Edcamp Philly. Accessible at http://www.edcampphilly .org/

3. **Edcamp Foundation:** A community owned and managed by the #Edcamp foundation for the purpose of educators' collaboration for organizing Edcamps. Accessible at http:// edcamp.org

4. **Hack Education or ISTE Unplugged:** A website to inform and question educators interested in social media, technology, teaching, and learning to build and participate in "unplugged"-style activities as a part of the ISTE (International Society for Technology in Education) conference each year. Accessible at http://www.isteunplugged.com/

Chapter 7

1. **Ning:** An online platform to build communities of people with a common interest. Accessible at http://ning.com

2. **The Educator's PLN:** A Ning community with the specified interest of collaborating to build a Personal Learning Network (PLN). This site is owned and managed by Tom Whitby. Accessible at http://edupln.com

3. **ISTE14Ning:** This is a Ning community set up in advance of the National ISTE 2014 Conference. Accessible at http:// 2014conference.ning.com/

4. **NYSCATE Ning:** New York State Association for Computers and Technology in Education. Accessible at http://nyscate .ning.com/

5. **Edutopia Groups:** This is a community that welcomes all teachers, administrators, parents, and others who are passionate about improving education. Accessible at http:// www.edutopia.org/groups

6. **English Companion-Ning:** A Ning community for English teachers. This site is owned and managed by James Burke. Accessible at http://englishcompanion.ning.com/

7. **The National Council for Social Studies-Ning:** A Ning community for Social Studies Educators. Accessible at http://ncssnetwork.ning.com/

8. **The Synapse-Ning:** A Ning community of Biology teachers. Accessible at http://thesynapse.ning.com/

9. **TechinEDU:** A Ning Community of Education Technology Educators. Accessible at http://techinedu.com/

10. **Flipped Learning Network:** A professional learning Ning community for teachers using screencasting in education. Accessible at http://flippedclassroom.org/main/

11. **EFL Classroom 2.0:** This Ning site is an effort to allow EFL (English as a foreign language) English language teachers to get low cost ELT (English language teaching) materials created by working teachers like themselves. Accessible at http://community.eflclassroom.com/

12. **Edmodo:** A website supported by Edmodo to introduce and explain the application to teachers. A video is available. Accessible at http://edmodo.com

KEY VOCABULARY

Blog: A site where a user creates posts to reflect or share information

Chat: A real-time discussion in Twitter using hashtags to curate tweets for the chat

Direct Message/DM: A private message sent in Twitter. The sender and receiver must be following each other to send and receive a DM

Favorite: Favorite is a way of saving a particular tweet to a favorite file for future retrieval

#FF: Hashtag Follow Friday. A hashtag used on Twitter to share names of people and sites that provide value to your learning that you want others to follow

Follow: The act of subscribing to a social media user's account (i.e., see their tweets, follow on Facebook, etc.)

Handle: The term used to describe a user's screen name on Twitter or other social networking sites

Hashtag: A combination of letters and/or numbers preceded by a hash symbol. This is the universal way to group tweets together on Twitter. Tweets sent out with a hashtag can be seen by anyone searching for that hashtag

Lists: A method of categorizing users on Twitter, organized by topic or subject

Lurk: To utilize a social media resource (such as Twitter) without actually participating (i.e., by sending a tweet, participating in a Twitter chat, etc.)

Mention: A tweet that contains the username (@username) anywhere in the tweet, thereby "mentioning" that user

MT: Shorthand for "modified tweet"

Ning: A social networking service that allows for the creation of communities around specific topics

Profile: Identifying information related to a social media user, usually containing a short biography and picture

ReTweet/RT: To repeat or copy (word for word) someone else's tweet

Spam: Unwanted advertising or a pitch appearing on the timeline

Timeline: The stream of messages a person gets from people being followed on Twitter, also called a Twitter Stream.

Trend/Trending: Tweets that are popular among large groups of users. Trends can be found at http://search.twitter.com page.

Tweet: 140-character message used to send information within Twitter

Twitter stream: The stream of messages a person gets from people being followed on Twitter, also called a Timeline

Unfollow: When a person stops following a person on Twitter. No notification is given to the person no longer followed

URL Shortener: A third-party service that shortens long URLs so they are easier to share and use. Common examples are found at https://bitly.com/ and http://goo.gl/

COMMONLY USED
EDUCATION TWITTER HASHTAGS

This is a link to a complete list of existing Twitter Education Hashtags: http://www.teachthought.com/twitter-hashtags-for-teacher/

#21CL	21st Century learner
#arted	Art Education
#artsed	Arts in Education
#atpeeps	Assistive Device in Ed supporters
#blogmust	Recommended blog post
#comments4kids	Please comment on student blog posts
#digped	Digital Pedagogy
#earlyed	Early Childhood Education
#edapp	Educational Apps
#edchat	Consistent hashtag covering all issues involving education
#edreform	Educational reform or change
#edtech	Educational technology
#educoach	Educational coaches/ instructional coaches
#elearn	Learning through cyber or virtual means
#FF	Follow Friday—Tweets recommending people to follow on Twitter

#flipclass	Teachers using a flipped instruction approach
#fliplearning	Content related to flipped teaching
#gbl	Game-based learning
#grammar	Tweets related to grammar, spelling, punctuation
#kidlit	Literacy for children
#mlearn	Mobile learning (cell phones, tablets)
#ocw	Open courseware
#openedu	Open education
#pblchat	Resources around Project-Based learning all the time
#pd	Professional development (also #profdev, #cpd, #td)
#pegeeks	Physical Education teachers
#pln	Personal/professional learning network
#rwworksop	Reading/Writing workshop
#sigetc	Educational Technology Coaches
#SLPeeps	Speech/Language Pathologists
#sm	Social media (Twitter, Facebook, LinkedIn, etc.)
#speced	Special Ed
#STEM	Science, Technology, Engineering, Math
#TT	Teacher Tuesday, make recommendations of teachers to follow on Twitter

CORWIN
A SAGE Company

The Corwin logo—a raven striding across an open book—represents the union of courage and learning. Corwin is committed to improving education for all learners by publishing books and other professional development resources for those serving the field of PreK–12 education. By providing practical, hands-on materials, Corwin continues to carry out the promise of its motto: **"Helping Educators Do Their Work Better."**